It's another Quality Book from CGP

This book is for 7-11 year olds.

Whatever subject you're doing it's the same
old story — there are lots of facts and you've just got
to learn them. KS2 Science is no different.

Happily this CGP book gives you all that important
information as clearly and concisely as possible.

It's also got some daft bits in to try and make the whole
experience at least vaguely entertaining for you.

What CGP is all about

Our sole aim here at CGP is to produce the highest quality
books — carefully written, immaculately presented and
dangerously close to being funny.

Then we work our socks off to get them out to you
— at the cheapest possible prices.

Published by Coordination Group Publications Ltd.

Illustrated by Sandy Gardner: illustrations@sandygardner.co.uk, Lex Ward and Ashley Tyson

Coordinated by Paddy Gannon

Contributors:
Erik Blakeley
Paul Burton
Chris Dennett
Paddy Gannon
Theo Haywood
Ed Lacey
Kate Stevens
Nick White

Updated by:
Taissa Csáky
Chris Dennett
Dominic Hall
Tim Major
James Paul Wallis

ISBN: 978 1 84146 270 7

Groovy website: www.cgpbooks.co.uk
Jolly bits of clipart from CorelDRAW®
Printed by Elanders Hindson Ltd, Newcastle upon Tyne.

Text, design, layout and original illustrations © Richard Parsons. 1999
All rights reserved.

Dead or Alive, Alive-o...

Animals and plants are called *living organisms*. Although *living things* look different from each other, they *all do the four life processes*. Something is only *alive* if it does all four processes.

Four Life Processes — All Living Things Do Them

1) Movement — even just a bit

Animals usually move their *whole bodies*, moving from one place to another (e.g. a bird flying).
Leaves and flowers turn *towards light* (e.g. a sunflower turning towards the Sun).

2) Reproduction — living things have offspring

Animals have babies (e.g. pigs have piglets).
Plants have seeds which turn into new plants (e.g. new oak trees grow from acorns).

3) Nutrition — taking in food

Food is used to provide energy.
Green plants make their own food using sunlight. Animals eat plants or other animals (e.g. eagles eat rabbits — *if they can catch them*).

4) Growth — it's all getting bigger

Seedlings grow into bigger plants.
Babies grow into adults.

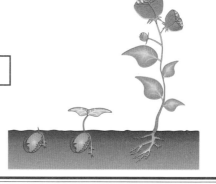

Are you alive — take a life test...

If it's alive it does all *four* of those *life processes*, whether it's a plant, a person or even a penguin. So do you know what the four are yet? If that was a "no", look back and get them remembered. Make sure you know the fancy words as well like "nutrition" and "reproduction".

Teeth and Eating

Teeth help you to *cut*, *tear* and *crush* your food before you swallow it. Humans are *omnivores* (they eat plants and animals) and their teeth are designed to eat most types of food.

Humans have three types of teeth

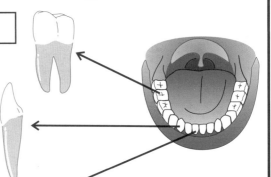

MOLARS:
> Back teeth for *crushing* and *grinding* food.

CANINES *(Fangs)*:
> In meat-eating animals like cats and dogs they are long and sharp and are used for *stabbing* and *gripping* food.

INCISORS:
> Front teeth are for *snipping* and *cutting* food.

> In our life we get two sets of teeth. MILK teeth are used from six months to about 5 years old then PERMANENT teeth replace them.

Teeth are different in other animals

CARNIVORES *(meat eaters)* have teeth suited to *killing* other animals and *tearing* flesh. Canines are long and pointed for *holding* and *gripping* flesh. Molars can *crack* and *crush* bones.

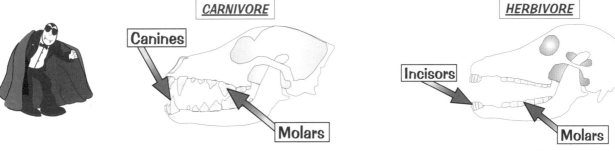

CARNIVORE

Canines

Molars

HERBIVORE

Incisors

Molars

HERBIVORES *(plant eaters)* have teeth suited to eating plants. Incisors *cut*. Molars *grind*.

Four ways to look after your teeth

> Brushing twice a day helps remove plaque. Fluoride toothpaste strengthens teeth.

> Flossing removes plaque and bits of food that bacteria feed on. Finally there's everyones favourite — a trip to the DENTIST!

> Eat sensible things like fruit and veg. Drinking milk is also good and some areas have flouride in the water.

Get your teeth into this lot...

What a fantastic page on choppers — lots of jolly pictures to make learning about teeth *dead easy*. But you really should know all about this already. Anyone with any sense knows how to look after their teeth, you'd miss them if they weren't there. Now smile....

Teeth and Eating

The Right Food is important for a Healthy Body

1) You need to eat a _balanced diet_.

2) A balanced diet is a _mixture_ of these _seven_ food types:

Food group	Why you need them	Which Foods have them
Carbohydrates 1) Starches	For energy	Bread Pasta Cereals Rice
Carbohydrates 2) Sugars (you need very little of this)		Biscuits Cakes Sweets
Proteins	For cell growth and repair	Fish Meat Milk Eggs
Fats	For energy	Milk, Cheese Butter Cooking oil Meat
Vitamins and Minerals	For healthy cells	Fruit Vegetables Dairy products
Fibre	Helps food move through the gut	Wholegrain bread Cereals Fruit Vegetables
Water	70% of the body is water	Drinks (and some foods)

Taking Health Risks can Damage the Body

Smoking
This causes heart attacks, blocked arteries, lung cancer and breathing problems. Nicotine in tobacco is addictive.

Solvents
Sniffing glue and paint damages the brain and is addictive. Solvent abuse, like drugs and alcohol, can cause mental problems.

Lack of Exercise
Lack of exercise weakens muscles including the heart and lungs. Exercise can burn up fat.

Alcohol
It slows down your reactions. Heavy drinking damages the liver, heart and stomach.

Drugs
These can kill you if misused. Many are addictive.

Live long — and prosper....
This page is all about staying _healthy_ and you'll be much better off if you learn it all. Eating a varied and _balanced diet_ is a good start. Keep well clear of dangerous drugs, solvents, smoking and drinking — they all _damage_ your body. Now get down and do 20 push-ups...

Keeping Healthy

The Major Organs of the Human Body

An *organ* is a part of the body that does a *special job*. Organs are all made up of *tiny cells*. On this monster of a diagram are some of the more important organs of the human body and the jobs they do.

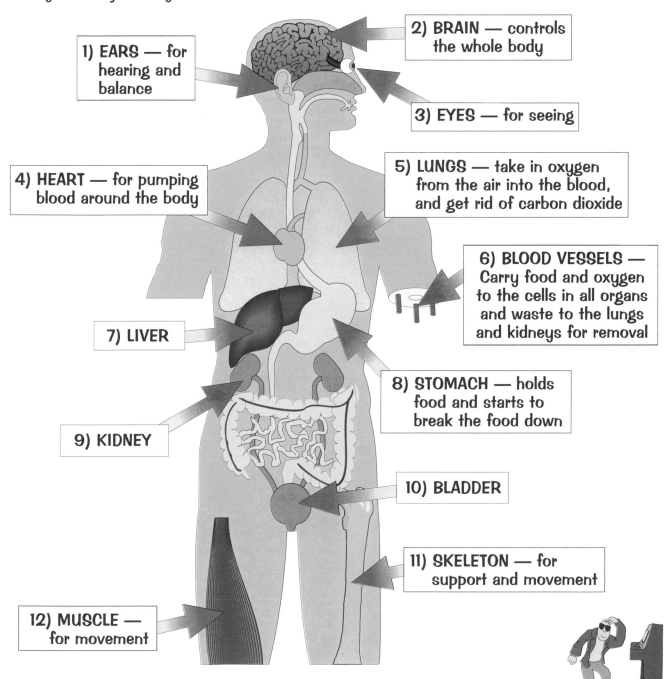

1) EARS — for hearing and balance

2) BRAIN — controls the whole body

3) EYES — for seeing

4) HEART — for pumping blood around the body

5) LUNGS — take in oxygen from the air into the blood, and get rid of carbon dioxide

6) BLOOD VESSELS — Carry food and oxygen to the cells in all organs and waste to the lungs and kidneys for removal

7) LIVER

8) STOMACH — holds food and starts to break the food down

9) KIDNEY

10) BLADDER

11) SKELETON — for support and movement

12) MUSCLE — for movement

Organs — harder to learn than pianos....

I know you want to do well, but I didn't say it would be easy. Twelve different things to learn is a lot, so take *two* organs at a time and learn everything about them — *where* they are and *what* they're for. Then take another two organs and do the same. In no time at all you'll have sussed out all the bits of the body and what they do.

Keeping Healthy

The Heart Pumps the Blood Around the Body

Circulatory system sounds like city traffic, but it's your *blood*, your *blood vessels* and your *heart* — and it's really important. Learn these facts:

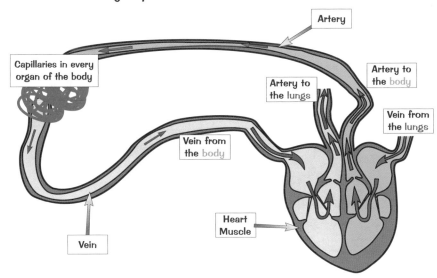

When the heart beats, blood is pumped out of two arteries. We've shown the one that carries blood to the body. The other takes blood to the lungs.

BLOOD VESSELS:
- Arteries — carry blood away from the heart to the body cells.
- Veins — carry blood away from the cells back to the heart.
- Capillaries — allow food and gases to move in and out of the blood.

1) One *artery* takes the blood to the lungs to pick up *oxygen*.

2) The other artery then takes the blood with *oxygen* and *food* to all the body cells.

3) The heart is inside the *rib cage*, which protects it.

4) When you exercise, the heart beats more often and pumps more blood with each beat.

The Lungs are big Air Sacs

1) The lungs are like two *spongy bags* filled with millions of tiny air sacs.

2) It's the job of the lungs to give *oxygen* to the blood and remove *carbon dioxide*.

3) This happens every time you breathe *in* and *out*.

4) When you exercise you breathe deeply and more often.

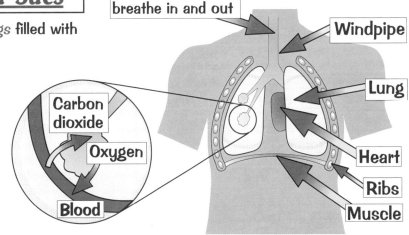

Heart beat — it's the rhythm of life....

Poets say our hearts make us fall in love and that time can heal a broken heart. *We* know that the heart is a big *pump* that moves our *blood* around the body. If it really breaks and stops pumping we have very little time left to do *anything*. You must look after your heart if it is to last for a long lifetime. Be active, be happy, *DON'T SMOKE...*

Moving and Growing

You have a Skeleton on the inside of your Body

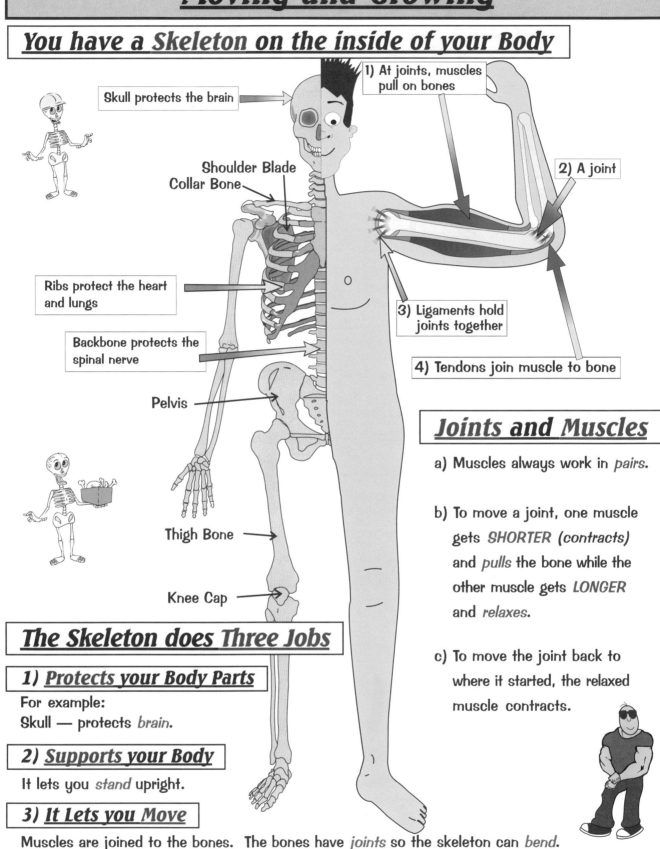

Skull protects the brain

1) At joints, muscles pull on bones

2) A joint

Shoulder Blade
Collar Bone

Ribs protect the heart and lungs

3) Ligaments hold joints together

Backbone protects the spinal nerve

4) Tendons join muscle to bone

Pelvis

Thigh Bone

Knee Cap

Joints and Muscles

a) Muscles always work in *pairs*.

b) To move a joint, one muscle gets *SHORTER* (contracts) and *pulls* the bone while the other muscle gets *LONGER* and *relaxes*.

c) To move the joint back to where it started, the relaxed muscle contracts.

The Skeleton does Three Jobs

1) Protects your Body Parts

For example:
Skull — protects *brain*.

2) Supports your Body

It lets you *stand* upright.

3) It Lets you Move

Muscles are joined to the bones. The bones have *joints* so the skeleton can *bend*.

This is alright — only got to learn the bare bones...

Without your skeleton you'd be a squishy bag of organs. Make sure you learn how we move our bodies. Muscles work in *pairs* — one *relaxes* while the other *contracts*. Think about it, and you should see how it works. Try watching the muscles in your arm move it up and down.

Section One — Life Processes and Living Things

Life Cycles

Reproduction produces Babies

1) Animals do not live for ever. More must be made to take the place of those that die.
2) Animals and humans are produced by *reproduction*.
3) Humans *don't lay eggs* but we all started off as an egg *inside* our mother.
4) When the egg is *fertilised* by a *sperm* from the father a tiny *ball of cells* called an *embryo* starts to develop.
5) The embryo grows inside the *womb* of the mother and becomes a *baby*.

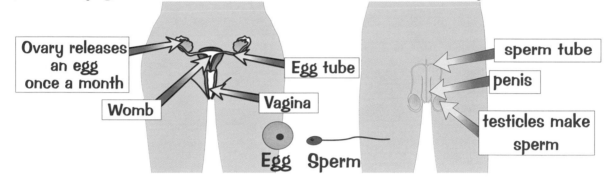

Life Cycle of a Human

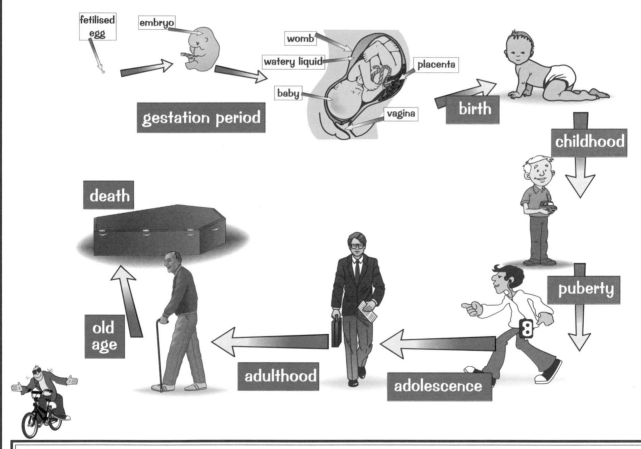

Life cycles — from cradle to grave, by bike...

The thing to remember here is that *new* animals have to be born, or there won't be any left when the old ones die. Remember, animals *change* as they grow. Tiny babies are totally dependent on their parents for everything, but you can do quite a bit for yourself, I should hope.

Helping Plants Grow Well

Built to do Four Life Processes

There are *four main parts to a plant*, all made to do those four life processes (see P.1).

To *GROW* plants need *light* and *warmth* and plenty of *water*.

1) Flowers

— necessary for *REPRODUCTION*.

They have *colour* and *smell* to attract insects. They make *pollen (male sex cells)* which join to the *eggs (female sex cells)*. Part of the flower dies and what's left becomes the new fruit with *seeds*.

2) Leaves

— necessary for *NUTRITION (feeding)*.

The *green stuff* in the leaves uses sunlight to change carbon dioxide gas and water into *food* — this is called *photosynthesis*.

3) Stem

— necessary to *HOLD* and *MOVE* the plant up towards the light.

It carries *water* and *minerals* from the *roots* to the *rest of the plant*.

4) Roots

— these *ANCHOR THE PLANT* to the ground so it doesn't blow away.

They also *soak* in *water* and *minerals* from the soil. The roots are therefore necesary for *NUTRITION (feeding)*.

Root hairs

Helping Plants Grow Well

The Plant Life Cycle has Four main Stages

1) Germination

1) Germination is when the *seed* starts to *grow*.

2) The seed cracks and tiny *roots* and *shoots* appear and grow into a new plant.

2) Pollination

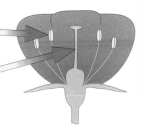

The stamens contain pollen grains

The carpel contains the eggs

1) The flower contains the reproductive organs.

2) The *male sex cells* (the pollen) are produced in the stamen.

3) The *female sex cells* (the eggs) are produced in the carpel.

4) *Pollination* is the process of getting pollen from the stamen to the carpel.

5) Some plants are pollinated by *insects* and others are pollinated by the *wind*.

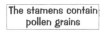

wind

3) Fertilisation and Seed Production

1) When the *pollen* grain joins with the *egg* it is called *fertilisation*.

2) The fertilised egg becomes a *seed*.

3) The flower *dies* and leaves behind a *fruit* with seeds.

4) These seeds will grow into new plants.

4) Seed Dispersal

1) The fruits and seeds are carried away from the parent plant to stop *overcrowding*.

2) *Animals* disperse the seeds when they eat the fruit.

3) The *wind* also carries the seeds away.

Plants — there's more to them than pretty flowers...

The name of the game here is to *learn* everything on these two pages — there's no easy way to say it I'm afraid. Take *one* part of the plant at a time and learn which of the life processes it's built to do. *Cover up* the picture of the life cycle and see how much you can *remember*. Enjoy.

Adaptations

Humans can live all over the world. We can do this because we are able to wear clothes and build houses suited for very different conditions — like Africa or the Arctic. Most plants and animals can only live in certain *environments* or surroundings — they can't change their clothes.

Where a Plant or Animal Lives is called its Habitat

The *habitat (where they live)* provides the plant or animal with *food* and *shelter*. The habitat also lets living things produce offspring *(make babies)* in a safe environment, e.g. a hedge, field or tree. The environment needs to be protected because if the habitat changes then the animal might die out.

OTHER EXAMPLES: *The Frog in a Pond Habitat:*   *A Bird in a Wood Habitat:*

Lots of lovely *slugs* to eat.   Plenty of materials to build a *nest*.
Water for frog spawn.   Feathers *camouflaged*.
Damp air so frog doesn't dry out.   Lots of juicy *worms* in the undergrowth.

Animals and Plants are Adapted to their Habitat

To help them to *survive* in their habitat, living things have developed *special features* to suit the place they live. These help them to survive in their habitat. Examples of adaptation:

The Otter

1) *Eyes* and *nostrils* can close under water.

2) *Webbed feet* help the otter move in water.

3) *Long whiskers* feel vibrations in water help it to find food.

The Squirrel

1) *Long claws* for gripping help it climb.

2) *Strong teeth* for opening nuts.

3) *Bushy tail* for balance.

The Cactus

1) *Long roots* find water.

2) *Fleshy stems* store water.

3) *Thin needle leaves* don't lose water.

Adaptations

Surviving Hot Environments — The Desert Rat

The roasty toasty and *baking hot* Sahara Desert can reach temperatures of up to 55°C
(30°C is about as hot as it gets in the middle of summer in the U.K. — if you're lucky).
The desert rat has these adaptations that let it live in the desert habitat successfully:

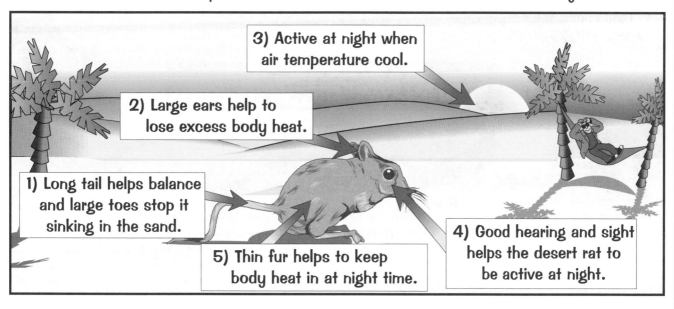

3) Active at night when air temperature cool.

2) Large ears help to lose excess body heat.

1) Long tail helps balance and large toes stop it sinking in the sand.

5) Thin fur helps to keep body heat in at night time.

4) Good hearing and sight helps the desert rat to be active at night.

Surviving Cold Environments — The Seal

The North Pole environment is well cold and I mean *cold*. It doesn't get warm, even in summer.
The seal is suited to the cold — these features let it live there successfully:

1) Streamlined body helps with swimming.

2) Small ears stop heat loss.

3) Layers of fat keep the body warm.

5) They have oily fur to keep them waterproof.

4) Webbed feet help movement through water.

Learn these habitats — make it a habit...

Animals have to be *adapted* for where they live, otherwise they might die. Imagine what would happen to a desert rat in the Arctic or a seal in the Sahara desert. Remember, *habitat* means *where* a plant or animal lives. Habitats can be large (e.g. a forest), or small (e.g. under a stone).

Habitats

There may be many different kinds of animals and plants living side by side in the same *habitat*. They all need food for energy and growth. Plants will get their food from the sunlight, the air and water, but animals have to eat other living things like plants or other animals.

Food Chains — Living Things Feeding on other Living Things

In food chains the arrows show what is being eaten by what, or what is *FOOD FOR* which animal.

Remember 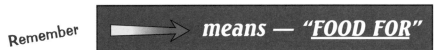 **means — "FOOD FOR"**

| Lettuce | Slug | Thrush | Hawk |

The lettuce is *food for* the slug.

The slug is *food for* the thrush.

The thrush is *food for* the hawk.

Food Chains use Wonderful Words

Remember these important parts of the food chain:

1) Plants are the Producers

They *produce (make)* their own food.

2) Animals are the Consumers

They get their food by *consuming (eating)* plants or other animals.

In this food chain:
The rose plant is the *producer* and the greenfly, the blue tit and the hawk are all *consumers*.

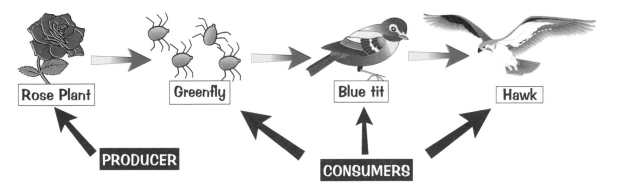

| Rose Plant | Greenfly | Blue tit | Hawk |

PRODUCER

CONSUMERS

Who's eating who — food for thought...

Food chains are all about what eats what. Thinking of *plants* as *producers* and *animals* as *consumers* seems a bit odd to begin with, but if you remember that plants are the *only* ones who *produce* their *own food*, you'll get it sorted no trouble at all. Don't forget that *all* the animals are consumers, even the ones that get eaten, because they *don't* produce their own food. Remember that the arrow in a food chain doesn't mean *"eats"* — it means *"is food for"*.

Habitats

Keys Unlock Information

Scientists use keys to *identify* unknown plants or animals, (and also to get in and out of their houses...). A key is a series of *questions*, each with *two* possible answers. The answers lead you to the next question or will identify the unknown creature. It's all very clever, as you'll find out when you give it a try...

Three Top Tips for Using Keys

1) Take *one* creature at a time.

2) Start at question (1) and go through the questions for *that creature only*.

3) *Follow* the *answers*. They lead you to the next question, or will identify the creature.

Have a go at using this key. Identify which group each of these animals is in.

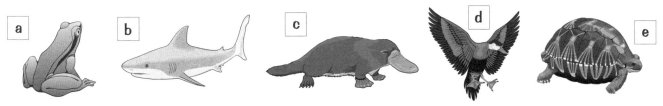

| 1) Does it have fins? | YES — it's a **FISH**
NO — go to (2) | 3) Does it have fur or hair? | YES — it's a **MAMMAL**
NO — go to (4) |
| 2) Does it have feathers? | YES — it's a **BIRD**
NO — go to (3) | 4) Does it have dry scaly skin? | YES — it's a **REPTILE**
NO — it's an **AMPHIBIAN** |

Answers: a = amphibian, b = fish, c = mammal, d = bird, e = reptile

Branched Keys

The key can be shown as a branched pattern. For ones like this you just follow the line. Try it.

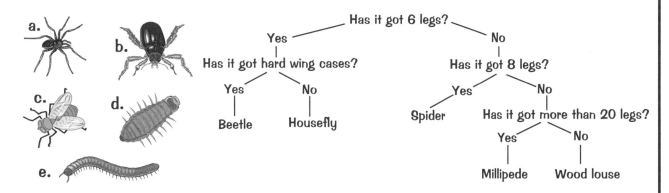

Answers: a = spider, b = beetle, c = housefly, d = wood louse, e = millipede.

Use keys — and unlock the answers...

You probably won't be expected to draw a key but you need to be able to *follow* one through and *identify* some unknown creatures. It's pretty *easy* really — just remember the *tips* above. Do remember to go through the key *step by step*, and *don't* just look at the pictures and *guess*.

Micro-Organisms

Micro-organisms are Tiny Living Things

1) *Micro-organisms* or microbes can only be seen through a *microscope*.
2) There are millions of micro-organisms in the *soil*, *air*, *water* and even the *human body*.
3) Some micro-organisms are *USEFUL* and some are *DANGEROUS*.
4) Bacteria and viruses are *micro-organisms*.

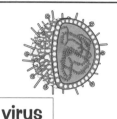

virus

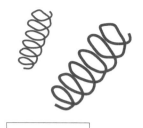

bacteria

The non-scientific word for these is *"germ"*

Helpful Micro-organisms do Important Jobs

2) Bacteria rot down dead organisms and put nutrients in the soil for plants to help them grow.

1) Bacteria help make cheese and yoghurt.

(Gee — I'm glad the world's not cluttered with dead bodies!)

3) Yeast is a micro-organism: it's used to make bread and beer.

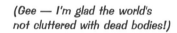

Harmful Micro-organisms can cause Disease

1) They cause *disease* and *illness*: flu, colds, measles, chicken pox, AIDS, tetanus, etc.
2) Micro-organisms cause *tooth decay*.
3) Micro-organisms can cause food to go *mouldy*.

Four Ways of Spreading Disease

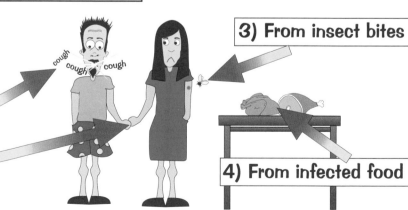

1) From coughs and sneezes

2) From touching infected people or objects

3) From insect bites

4) From infected food

Micro-Organisms

In the Kitchen — Be Sensible with Food

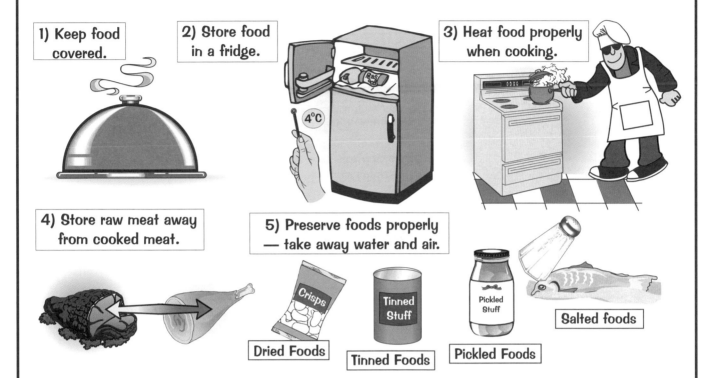

1) Keep food covered.

2) Store food in a fridge.

4°C

3) Heat food properly when cooking.

4) Store raw meat away from cooked meat.

5) Preserve foods properly — take away water and air.

Crisps

Dried Foods

Tinned Stuff

Tinned Foods

Pickled Stuff

Pickled Foods

Salted foods

Be Sensible with Personal Hygiene

1) Wash your hands after going to the toilet.

2) Don't sneeze or cough over people.

cough!

X

At the Doctors — Medicines are used to Fight Microbes

Medicines called vaccines and antibiotics are taken as pills or injected — to fight micro-organisms that cause illness.

Micro-organisms and disease — my favourite topic...

It's important that you know how diseases are caused, it'll help stop you from getting ill for one thing. Like it says, fighting disease in the home is all about being *sensible*. Remember that micro-organisms breed very fast in things that are *warm* and open to the *air*. Don't forget, not all micro-organisms are *harmful* — some are actually very *useful* to us.

Protecting the Environment

Humans cause a lot of damage — *killing animals* and *destroying habitats*. Unless we want to live in a lifeless, horrible wasteland we need to protect living things and the *environment* they live in.

Without Protection Lots of Living Things will Die Out

The most famous example of an animal being completely wiped out by man is the *dodo* — a flightless bird that died out about 300 years ago.

Lots of other animals are close to going the same way unless we do something about it...

North Atlantic Cod are Disappearing Fast

So many cod have been caught in the sea around Scotland that the cod have to be protected now — here's how...

 1) *Laws limit* the amount of cod that can be caught.

 2) Nobody is allowed to catch *baby cod*.

 3) People can only use *nets with big holes* that let the baby cod escape.

Destroying Habitats Kills Loads of Things at Once

In Britain we are slowly using up all our *meadowland* for farming and building.

Using this land destroys the habitat for loads of *plants and insects*.

Without these plants and insects, *mice and voles* don't have enough food.

Without the mice and voles, *owls* don't have enough food.

We need to protect habitats or we mess up *whole food webs*, making things like owls an endangered species.

This weeks hot topic — do dodo's do odd doo doos?...

We kill living things in two ways — *directly* for *food*, or by *destroying habitats*. If we're not careful about it we can make things *extinct*. Learn this page and save our owls and cod.

Summary Questions for Section One

This is one mighty section — *all* you ever wanted to know about life and more. Now all you need to do is *learn it...* No expense has been spared in preparing some brilliant questions but you need to keep going over them *again* and *again*. They test your knowledge on the basic facts. Now then let's get on with it, shall we?

1) Name the four life processes.
2) Say *which type* of teeth does the job:
       a) snipping/cutting   b) crushing/grinding   c) tearing/gripping.
3) Give *four ways* of preventing tooth decay.
4) Name the *seven* food groups.
5) Give *two reasons* why exercise is important.
6) Smoking and alcohol are health risks. Which causes *lung cancer*, which damages the *liver*?
7) Which organ pumps blood around the body?
8) Which *gas* does blood *take* from the lungs and which gas does it *give* to the lungs?
9) What is the *name* of the tube that carries *gases* in and out of the lungs?
10) Why do you have a skeleton? Give *three* reasons.
11) Muscles always work in pairs. When one muscle contracts, what does the *other muscle* do?
12) Name the main *stages* of the life cycle of a human being.
13) Name four important bits of a plant.
14) In what *part* of the plant are the *reproductive organs* found?
15) To make a *seed*, an *egg* must join with what?
16) What is *germination*:
       a) *a country*   b) a *disease*   c) a seed *starting* to *grow*
17) What is the *name* of the *place* where a plant or an animal lives?
18) How is a cactus plant *adapted* to living in a *desert habitat*?
19) Give *one* adaptation that a desert rat has so it can survive in a *desert habitat*.
20) Give *one* adaptation that a seal has so it can live in *cold sea areas*.
21) In a *food chain* what do the arrows mean?
22) What type of organisms are always producers?
23) What do consumers eat?
24) Use the *key* to find out the names of each alien creature.

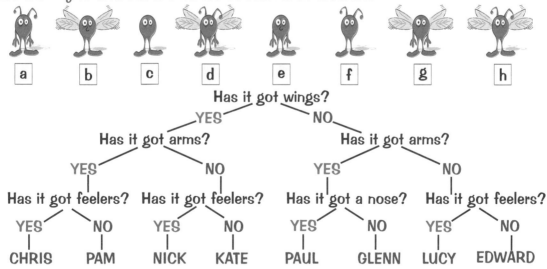

25) What is the *non-scientific* name often given to micro-organisms?
26) Give *three* examples of *helpful* micro-organisms.
27) Name two groups of *medicines* used by doctors to fight micro-organisms.
28) Why do we need to protect habitats?

Comparing Materials

Materials have certain PROPERTIES which make them Useful

You need to be able to describe and compare the properties of a material and say why it's used for a job. We use certain materials for certain jobs...

1) Because they are _STRONG_ (sturdy).

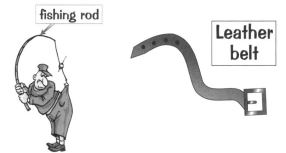

Steel bridge · Bleach · Plastic container

2) Because they are _HARD_ (difficult to scratch).

Diamond cutter · Metal hammer head

3) Because they are _FLEXIBLE_ (bendy)...

 fishing rod

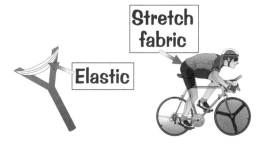

Leather belt

...OR _RIGID_ (stiff).

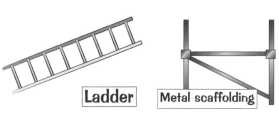

Ladder · Metal scaffolding

4) Because they are _TRANSPARENT_ (see-through)...

Glass

Fabric

...OR _OPAQUE_ (not see-through).

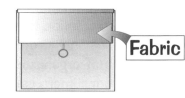

5) Because they can **STRETCH**...

Stretch fabric

 Elastic

...OR be _COMPRESSED_ (squashed).

Metal spring

Be strong, be tough — learn all these words...

It'd be _no good_ trying to dry yourself with a _plastic sheet_, or bang a nail in with a _cushion_, would it? We choose to use different materials to do different things because their special properties make them _right for the job_.

Conductors and Insulators of Heat

1) Some Materials let Heat Pass through them Easily

1) These materials are called *THERMAL CONDUCTORS*.
2) *METALS* are good *THERMAL CONDUCTORS*.
3) Because heat passes through them quickly
— metals normally feel *COLD*.

2) Some Materials Do Not let Heat Pass through them

1) Materials that do not let heat pass through them are called *THERMAL INSULATORS*.

Plastic kettle   **Cork pot stand**   **Wooden handle**   **Oven glove**   **Thermal vest**

2) Plastic, cork, wood and fabrics are good *THERMAL INSULATORS*.
3) Thermal insulators are good for keeping heat *OUT* as well as *IN*.

  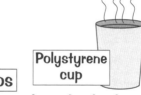

Cool box

Used to keep
food cool

Thermos

Polystyrene cup

Used to keep hot drinks hot
— and cold drinks cold.

A *GOOD INSULATOR* = A *POOR CONDUCTOR*

3) Heat Travels from a Warmer Material to a Colder one

HOT   COLD

HEAT

Heat is like a tourist — it loves to travel...

Remember that heat *only* moves from *hot* things to *colder* things, *never* the other way around. Some things let heat travel through them easily and others don't. Think of a saucepan — the heat goes through the *pan* to the food, but *not* through the *handle* to your fingers. Remember, the same material that keeps heat out of something can also keep heat in.

Conductors and Insulators of Electricity

1) Conductors let Electricity Flow through them

1) Materials that can carry electricity are called *conductors* — they *conduct* electricity.
2) *Metals* like copper, iron, steel and aluminium are all good conductors.

2) Insulators do not let Electricity Flow through them

1) Materials that can *not* carry electricity are called *insulators* — they don't conduct electricity.
2) Wood, plastic, glass and rubber are all insulators.

Wood

Plastic

Glass

Rubber

3) Insulators and Conductors both have Important Uses

WIRE

Plastic covering.
Electricity can't flow through —
so you won't get a shock if you handle it.

Copper wire allows electricity to
flow through — so watch out pal.

PLUG

Metal pins —
Conduct electricity

Insulated flex

Plastic —
Safe to hold

4) Electricity can be Dangerous

You shouldn't touch *anything* electrical with wet hands
— and that includes *switches*. Electricity can be
conducted through sweat (salty water) to your body,
giving you an electric shock, and that's no joke.

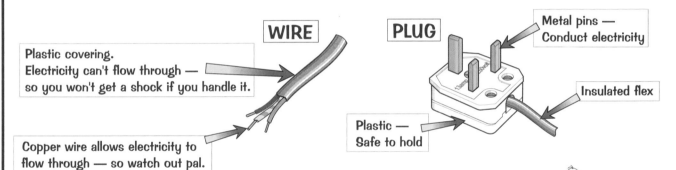

Beware
little mouse!!!

Plastic coating
(insulator)

Copper wire
(conductor)

Glass (insulator)

Wire (conductor)

Wood (insulator)

Learn about electricity — don't let it shock you...

You need to know which materials conduct electricity, and what materials are insulators.
Don't forget that mains electricity can be very *dangerous* — so make sure you watch out...

Rocks and Soil

Rocks are all around — underground, on beaches, in gardens, buildings, walls, quarries, cemeteries. That's why they're dead useful and have been for yonks...

Not All rocks are the same

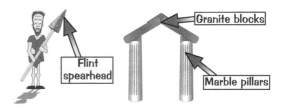

Flint spearhead

Granite blocks

Marble pillars

1) Some rocks are *HARDER*.

2) Some rocks are *SOFTER*.

3) Some rocks are *IMPERMEABLE*.

    (They DO NOT allow water to SOAK through).

4) Some rocks are *PERMEABLE*.

    (They allow water to SOAK through).

Marble   Slate

CHALK   LIMESTONE

Soil is made from Four things

WORN DOWN ROCK + HUMUS + AIR + WATER

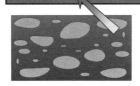

Humus is dead and rotting material.

Soils are Different because not all Rocks are the same

It depends what *kind* of *worn down rock* it comes from.

GRAVELLY SOIL
Full of small stones so water drains through quickly.

SANDY SOIL
Light and dry with air gaps so water drains through quickly.

CLAY SOIL
Very sticky when wet; a heavy soil. Water does not drain through quickly.

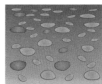

Like it or lump it — you need to know this stuff...

There's plenty of words here to learn, and some of them do look a bit long and complicated but you've got to know them. *Impermeable* means it's impossible for water to soak through, so *permeable* means water can flow through. Make sure you know the things that make up soil, not forgetting the *air* and *water* — they may not seem like much, but they're really important.

Properties of Solids, Liquids and Gases

Anything you can think of is either a solid, a liquid or a gas — or a mixture of these.

.......are easy to control

1) Solids can be cut or shaped.

2) The SHAPE and VOLUME of a solid <u>don't change</u> — unless you break a bit off.

3) Anything you can take hold of is solid.

**.........are more difficult to control
They keep wanting to run away!!**

1) Liquids are runny. They flow downwards.

2) The surface of a liquid in a container stays level.

4) The SHAPE of a liquid can <u>change</u> depending on the shape of the container it's in.

3) The VOLUME of a liquid <u>doesn't change</u>.

**....are very hard to control.
They keep wanting to escape!!**

1) Gases are all around us. Most gases are invisible.

2) Air is made of a mixture of different gases.

3) A gas in a container <u>completely fills the container</u>. It has the SAME SHAPE and the SAME VOLUME as the container.

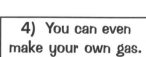

4) You can even make your own gas.

BURP!! Pardon me!!

5) A gas that's <u>not</u> in a container spreads out further and further — the VOLUME keeps <u>increasing</u>.

Solids, liquids and gases — three for the price of one...

It's important to *learn* all the little *details* on this page to make sure that you *really* know the difference between a solid, a liquid and a gas. Have a look at all the things around you and decide whether they're *solids*, *liquids* or *gases*.

Temperature & Water

Temperature — How Hot and Cold

1) *Temperature* tells you how *hot* or *cold* things are.
2) You *measure* temperature with a *thermometer*.
3) You measure *temperature* in *degrees celsius* — °C.

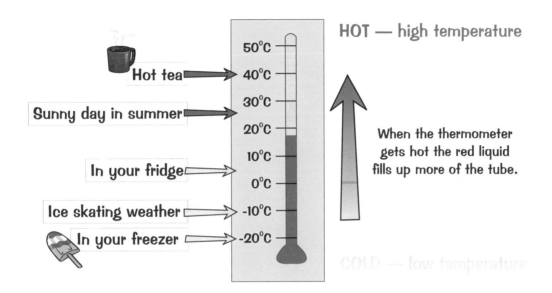

HOT — high temperature

50°C

Hot tea — 40°C

30°C

Sunny day in summer — 20°C

10°C

In your fridge — 0°C

Ice skating weather — -10°C

In your freezer — -20°C

When the thermometer gets hot the red liquid fills up more of the tube.

COLD — low temperature

Water Boils at 100°C and Freezes at 0°C

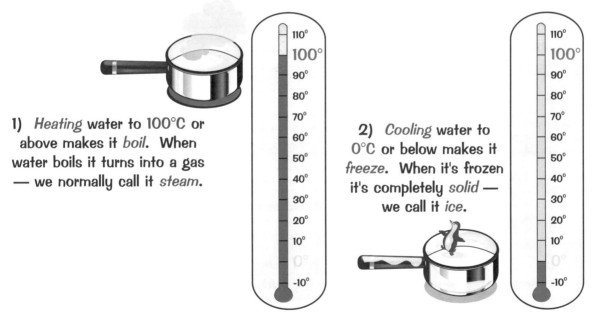

1) *Heating* water to 100°C or above makes it *boil*. When water boils it turns into a gas — we normally call it *steam*.

2) *Cooling* water to 0°C or below makes it *freeze*. When it's frozen it's completely *solid* — we call it *ice*.

3) Water is the *only liquid* which boils at 100°C and freezes at 0°C.

Don't get all steamed up about this — just chill out...

Thermometers *measure* temperature — which is handy if you're a weatherman. Don't forget that water always starts *boiling* when it gets to 100°C, and always starts *freezing* when it gets down to 0°C. Fancy a cup of tea? I'll just heat some liquid water to 100°C...

Reversible Changes

Some Changes are Reversible

In a *reversible* change a material turns into something that looks and feels different, but it isn't changed *forever*. The material can be *changed back* so it looks and feels the same as it did before.

These are *reversible changes*:

1) Water *turns into snow or ice* when it gets very cold. When it warms up it turns *back into water*.

chocolate

2) Chocolate goes *soft and gooey* if you heat it. When it cools down it *goes hard again*.

> The materials change back to how they were before.

Freezing and Melting are Reversible Changes

Heating a *solid* can make it change into a *liquid*. When this happens it's called MELTING.

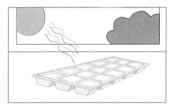

If you leave ice cubes in a warm place, say on a sunny window sill, they'll melt and turn into water.

Cooling the liquid turns it back into a solid. This is called FREEZING.

If you put the melted ice-cubes back in the freezer they'll turn into solid ice again.

Candle wax can melt and turn solid *over and over again* — because melting is a REVERSIBLE CHANGE.

When the wax gets hot it melts and turns into a liquid.

When the wax cools it turns back into a solid.

Reversible Changes

Dissolving is a Reversible Change

Some solids *dissolve* in liquid when you mix them together. It's a *reversible change*, because you can get the solid back.

1) Salt gets mixed up with water in a jar.

2) After stirring for a bit you can't *see* the salt anymore.

If you don't believe the salt's still there, taste the water ...

Euch!

YOU CAN *REVERSE* THE CHANGE AND GET THE SALT BACK

1) Heating the water gently will make it *evaporate* — that means it'll all dry out into the air. Leaving the jar on a warm radiator for a week or so should do the job nicely.

2) When all the water's dried out there are salt crystals left at the bottom of the jar. The change has been *reversed*.

There are two more types of reversible change — *evaporation* and *condensation*. There's more about them on *PAGE 29*.

Reversible Changes — they're a two way street...

You know that solids melt when they get hot enough, and then go back to solid when they're cooled back down — you've seen water *freezing* and ice *melting*. Don't forget, these changes *can* be *reversed*, the water won't be stuck as ice forever if you warm it up again.

The Water Cycle

The Water Cycle is Evaporation and Condensation of Water

1) The water here on planet Earth is constantly recycling. Strange but true...

2) When the temperature gets really low rain drops can fall as snow or hail instead of rain.

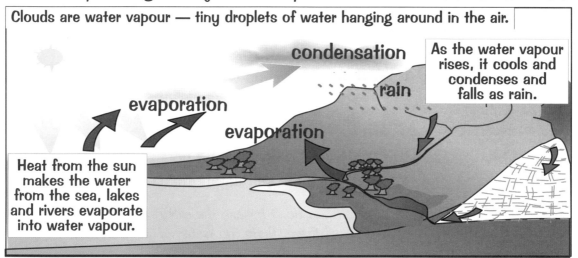

Clouds are water vapour — tiny droplets of water hanging around in the air.

condensation

rain

As the water vapour rises, it cools and condenses and falls as rain.

evaporation

evaporation

Heat from the sun makes the water from the sea, lakes and rivers evaporate into water vapour.

Evaporation — turning to a gas

1) The Sun can heat water. The water goes into the air — it doesn't disappear. The water *evaporates* into a gas.

Puddle

2) The water from wet clothes *evaporates* into the air.

A LIQUID *EVAPORATES* INTO A GAS WHEN IT IS *WARMED*

Condensation — turning from a gas back to a liquid

Cool mirror

Water vapour in hot air

Water droplets

1) Water vapour in the air *cools* and turns into water droplets.
2) The water vapour *condenses*.

A GAS *CONDENSES* INTO A LIQUID WHEN IT IS *COOLED*

Water Cycle — sounds like a cross-channel bike..

Remember that ice, water and steam are all *states* of water. You really do need to know the words *evaporation* and *condensation*. Don't forget that water *doesn't* disappear when it evaporates, but it turns into a gas. Look at the diagram of the water cycle at the top of the page really carefully, and try to *follow* the water on its way around the picture.

Dissolving

Soluble — will dissolve

1) Salt dissolves completely in water to make a *solution*.

2) Salt is *soluble* in water.

3) Other soluble substances *(materials)* include sugar and instant coffee.

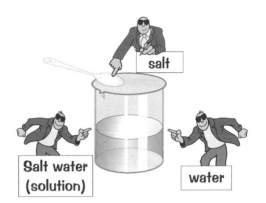

Insoluble — will not dissolve

1) Soil will *not dissolve* in water. Some soil will remain at the bottom *undissolved*.

2) The rest of the soil particles will float around in the water, but they won't dissolve — it's *insoluble* in water.

3) Other examples include wood, chalk, clay, sand, wax and oil.

There's a Limit to how much can Dissolve

When you add salt to water there comes a point when you *can't dissolve any more*.

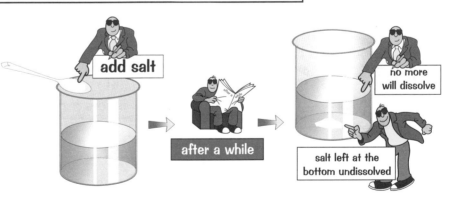

The amount of solid you can add before this happens is different for different solids.

Try and dissolve all this in your brain...

This is all about what dissolves and what doesn't. Don't forget that things *don't disappear* when they dissolve. They're still there — you just can't see them. I keep on saying it, but people keep on writing that things do disappear. Learn it.

Separating Solids and Liquids

Sieving — sorting out the Big Bits from the Small Bits

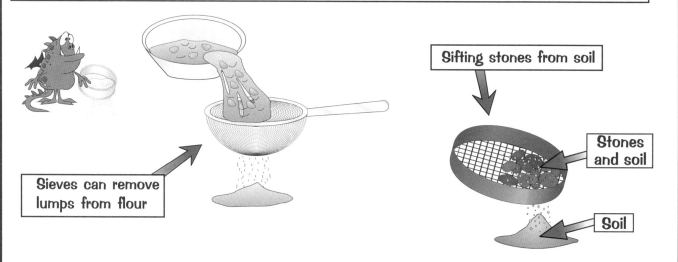

Sieves can remove lumps from flour

Sifting stones from soil

Stones and soil

Soil

Filtering — separating Solid bits from a Liquid

A colander can separate peas from boiling water.

A tea strainer keeps the tea leaves out of the cup of tea.

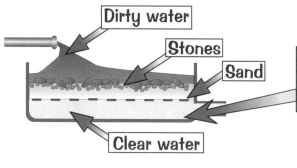

Dirty water

Stones

Sand

Clear water

Filter Beds are used to clean water. The dirty water is passed through a filter bed before it goes back to the river.

Filter paper can be used to separate very fine solids that are mixed with a liquid like water. The solids are not dissolved in the water and can't pass through the paper.

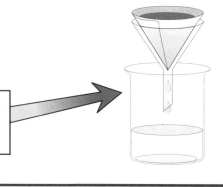

Separating Solids and Liquids

Evaporation — separating Soluble Solids from Water

With tea, the tea leaves can't pass through the holes in the tea bag, but the brown flavouring is dissolved in the water so it can. This is good for drinking the tea, but it's a problem if you want to separate the flavouring from the water. Follow the diagram to see what you do. Smashing fun.

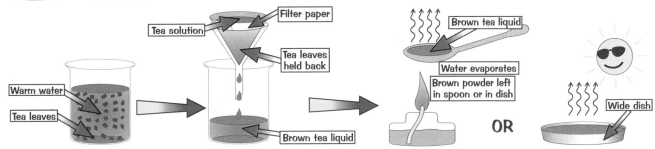

(You can heat and evaporate off the water by using a flame, or just put the water and solid in a wide dish and leave it in a warm place.)

Separating a Mixture of Salt, Sand and Water

The mixture is a *soluble solid (salt)*, an *insoluble solid (sand)*, and *water*.
To separate such a mixture of different materials you need to *filter* and *evaporate* the mixture.

1) FILTER   Filter the mixture of salt, sand and water to remove the *sand*.
The salty water then comes through the filter into a beaker.

2) EVAPORATE   The salt and water mixture is *warmed* to evaporate off the *water*.

3) CONDENSE   The water vapour must be *cooled* to turn it back into a *liquid*.

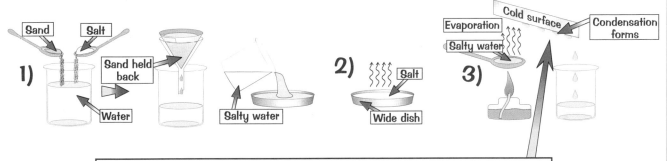

If you want the water and don't want it to be lost into the air, then you must collect it by CONDENSING it on a COLD SURFACE.

Mixtures — get 'em sorted...

You need to know what you've gotta do to *separate* solids from water. Remember, it depends on whether the solid's actually *dissolved* in the water.
And don't forget — things *don't disappear* when they dissolve, even though you cn't always see them. They're still there, so if you evaporate the liquid off, you'll get the solid back.

Irreversible Changes

An irreversible change lasts forever

In an *irreversible change*, a material turns into a *completely new and different material*. The new material *can't be changed back* into what it was before.

These changes are all *irreversible*:

1) Wood and paper *burn* to ash.

2) Flour, water and yeast are *baked* to make bread.

3) Dead plants and animals *decay* to humus.

4) Clay is *baked* into a pot.

You _can't_ change the materials _back_ to how they were before.

Irreversible changes are *incredibly useful*

Irreversible changes are very useful. Bread would be pretty *disgusting* if it could turn back into flour and water. Mugs would be completely useless if they turned *back into clay* when they got wet.

Some things _cook_ when you heat them —

and change completely

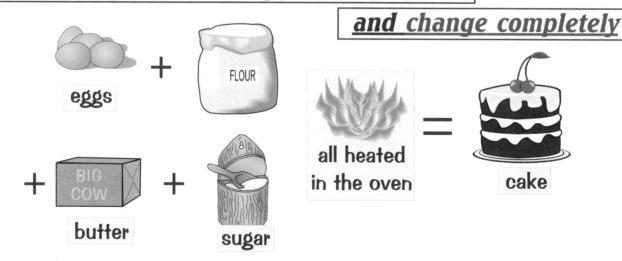

eggs + FLOUR

+ butter + sugar

all heated in the oven = cake

Cooking is a permanent change. It's irreversible.
You can't get the ingredients back again once you've cooked them.

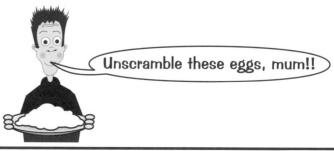

Unscramble these eggs, mum!!

Irreversible Changes

Some things burn when you heat them

When materials are *burned* they *change completely*.
You *can't reverse* changes made by *burning*.

Burning Fuel — an Important Irreversible Change

1) *Wood*, *coal* and *gas burn* to produce heat energy.

2) This can be converted (*changed*) into *electricity*.

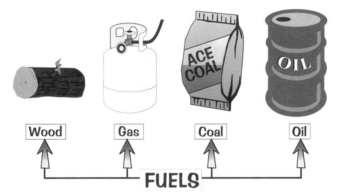

3) They can produce *light* as well which is jolly.

4) *Fuels* can *burn* to drive machines like cars.

5) Our bodies *burn* (*use up*) food slowly to give us *energy*.

Food

Irreversible Changes — they're a one way street, pal...

These are all changes that *can't* be undone. The chap at the bottom of the page over there won't get his eggs unscrambled because it's impossible. Think about things that change when you add them to water, like plaster of Paris, which goes *dead hard* and sets.

Summary Questions for Section Two

Try these. *Don't worry* if you get stuck. Look back through this section... but make sure you know them next time you try the questions.

1) Why would *steel* be used to make a *bridge?*

2) Name a material that is a good *thermal conductor.*

3) What is a *thermal insulator?*

4) Would *electricity* be able to pass through:
   a) Wood b) Metal c) Plastic?

5) Are all rocks the *same? Explain* your answer.

6) What does *permeable* mean?

7) What are the *three groups* that materials fall into?
   Solids, _____, _____.

8) Which of these are *reversible* changes and which are *irreversible?*
   a) water freezing   b) coal burning   c) ice cream melting   d) metal rusting.

9) Can you explain how *puddles* disappear?

10) I want to get *salt crystals* from a solution of *salt* and *water. How* do I do it?

11) "The water on planet Earth recycles all the time".
    Explain this statement.

12) Here are some pieces of *equipment* used to separate out messed up materials.

| Magnet | Filter paper & funnel | Sieve | Spoon and burner |

Match the *best* equipment to *separate* out the mixed up materials in a) to d).
You can only use *each* piece of equipment *once.*

   a)   stones and water
   b)   nails and talcum powder
   c)   sand and gravel
   d)   sugar and water

13) Name three different fuels.

14) What has to happen to fuels so that they can produce heat and light *energy?*

15) Name the *fuel* that the human *body* 'burns'.

Magnets

1) Only Metals are Attracted to Magnets

North Pole

South Pole

2) Some Magnets are Stronger than Others

This bar magnet holds more paperclips than the horseshoe — so it's *stronger*.

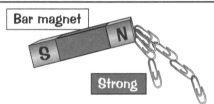

Bar magnet

Strong

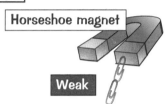

Horseshoe magnet

Weak

3) Not All Metals are Attracted to Magnets

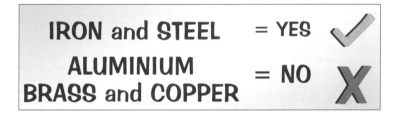

IRON and STEEL = YES ✓

ALUMINIUM
BRASS and COPPER = NO ✗

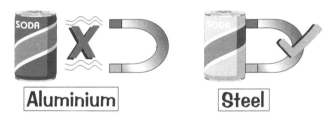

Aluminium

Steel

4) Magnets put a force on other Magnets or Magnetic Materials

1) A north and a south pole will *attract* each other.

magnets move towards each other

2) *Two* north poles will *repel* each other.

magnets move away from each other

3) *Two* south poles will *repel* each other.

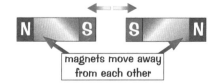

magnets move away from each other

Feel attractive — you must be a magnet...

Magnetism is a bit weird when you think about it — a magnet can pick up paperclips without even touching them... Remember, metals can be magnetic, but *not all* metals are magnetic. You need to get the difference between being magnetic and actually being a magnet straight in your mind. Think about two magnets *repelling* each other — *only* magnets can do that.

The Force of Friction and Air Resistance

Friction occurs when Two Surfaces Touch each other

1) Rougher surfaces slow things down a lot

Roads are rough to help you slow down quickly.

2) Smooth surfaces don't slow you down as much

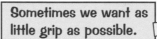

Sometimes we want as little grip as possible.

3) Friction gives us grip

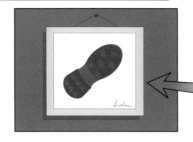

Without grip, starting and stopping is hard. That's why the soles of your trainers are such works of art.

4) Friction produces heat

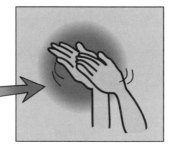

That's why, when you rub your hands together, they get warm.

Air Resistance Slows Down Moving Objects

1) Air slows you down as you move through it — just like trying to wade through *deep water* — only not nearly so bad.

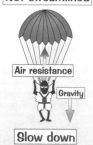
Not streamlined
Air resistance
Gravity
Slow down

2) To travel faster through air, things need to be *streamlined*.

3) To travel slower through air, you need a large *surface area* (like a parachute).

Streamlined
Speed up

Go on — Force yourself to get to grips with this section...

Friction acts when things touch and *air resistance* kinda slows you down when you move. Think about how easy or hard it is to *slide* on different surfaces. Don't forget, even though friction tends to slow things down it can be pretty *useful*. If there wasn't any friction everything would just slide out of your hands. Remember that the *bigger* the *area* you've got, the *more* air resistance you'll feel.

Gravity and Opposite Forces

You've learnt about two exciting forces with fancy names on the last page.
Now here's another one for you to learn — gravity.

Gravity pulls objects down towards the Centre of the Earth

1) Gravity pulls you down whether
you're in the air, in water, or
standing on the ground.

Gravity

"What goes up,
must come down".

2) *Wherever* you are on the Earth, things are
pulled down *towards the centre of the Earth*.

That's why it always rains towards the centre
of the Earth — and why you *can't fall off*.

Free at last!!!

3) The *size* of the gravitational force is pretty much
the *same* all over the Earth. You would have to be
a *very, very long* way from the Earth before you
no longer felt the effect of its gravitational pull.

When you push or pull there's an Opposite Force

1) When you push or pull something, you can feel an
opposite force pushing or pulling the *other way*.

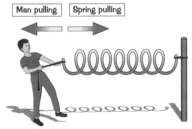

Man pulling   Spring pulling

2) The man is pulling on the spring,
and the spring is *pulling back*.

Man pushing   Wall pushing back

3) This bloke's pushing the wall,
but the wall is *pushing back*.

*I know it sounds a bit odd at first, but the
wall is pushing back. If it weren't pushing
back, it'd have to move or fall over.*

Gravity — very down-to-Earth...

Remember that gravity pulls us towards the centre of the Earth, so it keeps us stuck on the
Earth's surface. On the Moon, you feel the *Moon's gravity* rather than the Earth's. The Moon is
smaller than the Earth, so the force of gravity is *less* and you don't get pulled down as much.

Section Three — Physical Processes

The Earth and the Sun

The movement of the Earth in space gives us days and years — here's how:

The Earth takes one Year to Orbit the Sun

1) An orbit is the *path* an object takes through space around another object.

2) It takes *365¼ days (one year)* for the Earth to *orbit* the Sun.

3) The Earth is held in its orbit around the Sun by the Sun's *gravity (gravitational pull)*.

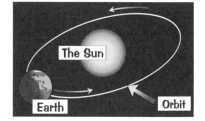

The Earth Rotates to give us Days and Nights

1) The Earth is roughly *spherical (round)*.

2) The Earth takes *24 hours* to rotate *(spin)* once on its axis. *(24 hours = 1 day)*.

3) The side of the Earth *facing* the Sun is lit up — so it's *daytime* for this side.

4) The side of the Earth facing *away* from the Sun is in darkness — so it's *night-time* for this side.

5) The Earth's axis is slightly *tilted*.

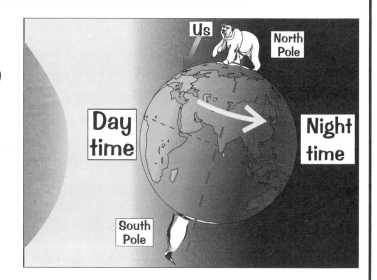

The Sun doesn't Move — it's Us that Move

Because the Earth is rotating, the Sun appears to move across the sky as the day goes by.

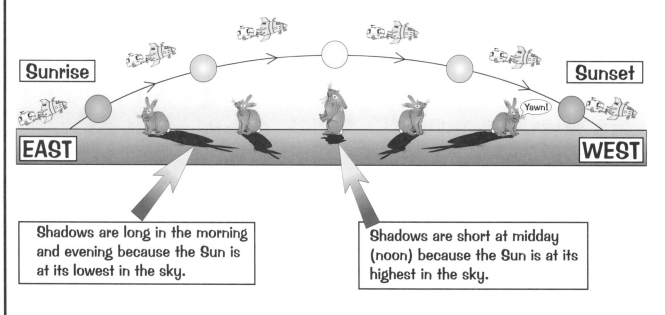

Shadows are long in the morning and evening because the Sun is at its lowest in the sky.

Shadows are short at midday (noon) because the Sun is at its highest in the sky.

The Moon

The Moon orbits the Earth

1) It takes about *28 days* for the Moon to orbit the Earth.

2) The Moon is held in its orbit around the Earth by the Earth's *gravitational pull*.

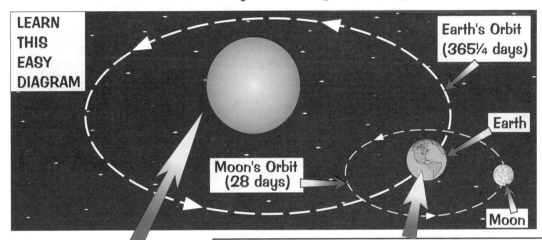

LEARN
THIS
EASY
DIAGRAM

Earth's Orbit
(365¼ days)

Earth

Moon's Orbit
(28 days)

Moon

The Sun is bigger than the Earth, so its gravitational pull is larger than the Earth's.

The Earth is bigger than the Moon, so its gravitational pull is larger than the Moon's — that's why astronauts can jump higher on the Moon than on the Earth.

The Moon Appears to change Shape as it orbits the Earth

This is because we *only see* the part of the Moon which is reflecting light from the Sun towards us — as the Moon orbits the Earth we see different amounts of the Moon's sunny side, so the Moon appears to change shape.

The dark side of the Moon is facing the Earth so we cannot see it — this is the *New Moon*.

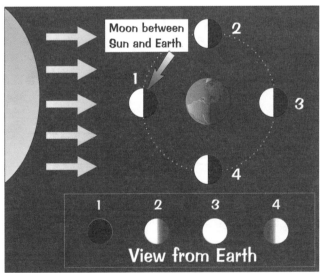

Moon between Sun and Earth

View from Earth

3

We can see all the sunlit side of the Moon — this is the *Full Moon*.

2 and 4

We can see half of the sunlit side of the Moon — this is the *Half Moon*.

Sun from dawn till dusk — just a perfect day...

There is quite a lot to learn here, but these are all the facts you'll need to know. I know people always talk about the Sun rising and setting as if it's the Sun that goes around the Earth, but it's *not*, it's the other way around. Remember *what's* orbiting what, and how *long* it takes.

Sources of Light

If you're feeling in the dark about light and how you see, then read on and all will be revealed.

Light Sources — Give Out Light

Light sources include: —

1) The Sun

2) Stars

3) Candle flame

4) Electric light

Some objects seem bright, but they are only *reflecting* light from elsewhere.
These are *NOT* light sources. These things include the Moon, planets, mirrors and shiny objects.

Remember:

Light source

Not light sources...

Light has Three Important Properties

1) Light travels in *straight lines* from a light source to your eyes.

2) If something is in the way you get a *shadow*. (See P. 39)

3) Light travels *very fast, about one million times faster than sound travelling in air.*

Shadows

Light *can pass through* some materials (such as *glass* and *air*),
but it *can't pass through* others (such as *wood, metal, stone, next-door's cat* and *you*).

When Light from a Source is Blocked — you get a Shadow

1) There's a *shadow* here because the *wall* blocks the Sun's light.

Light source

Light rays blocked by wall

This light ray goes over the top of the wall

HAAAAAAAYYYYAAAA!

Karate man also blocked by wall

Shadow

2) The more directly *overhead* the light source *(the Sun)* is, the *shorter* the shadow.

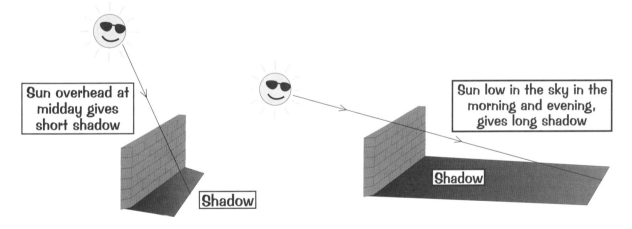

Sun overhead at midday gives short shadow

Sun low in the sky in the morning and evening, gives long shadow

Shadow

Shadow

3) The *closer* the light source to the object the *larger* the shadow.

Much too small!

Now that's more like it!

Shadows — don't be left in the dark...

Sources and sauces ...confusing...na..
Have a look at the shadow diagrams and *see* what's happening to the *rays of light* in each one.

Mirrors

1) Mirrors Reflect light Back at the same Angle

Light rays

Reflected light rays

If you put a mirror in the *right place*, you can even see around corners.
Look at the rays of light in the diagram below.

Mum's happy — she thinks Tom is learning Science *but* — view this happy scene from above.

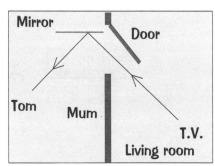

Scene from above.

Tom can see a fabulous program on TV, and thanks to the fact that light from the TV is reflected back at the same angle, Mum can't see it, so she doesn't suspect a thing....

2) Periscopes use a Pair of Mirrors to help see around Objects

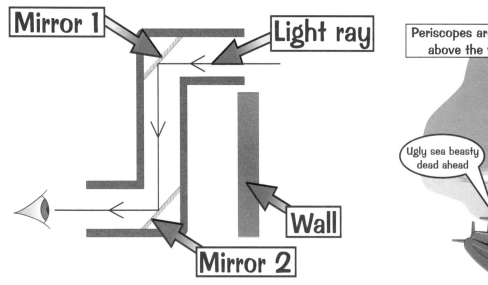

Mirror 1

Light ray

Wall

Mirror 2

Periscopes are used to see above the water level

Ugly sea beasty dead ahead

Mirrors — they'll help you reflect on this...

You can see that when light hits a mirror it bounces back off, and you get a *reflection*. If you use a mirror, you can see behind you or even around a corner. Follow the *light rays* in the diagrams if you're not sure. Also, don't forget the important rule — a light ray hitting a mirror is reflected back at the *same* angle.

How We See

We See things when Light from a Source Enters our Eyes

1) Light may come *directly* from the source to your eyes — like when you look at a *candle*.

In diagrams you put the arrow on the light ray *(light beam)* pointing away from the source and towards the eye.

2) Light also *bounces off* objects into your eyes — like when you look at a *cake*.

I NEED CAKES

Light Bounces off Some Materials Better than Others

1) *Mirrors* and *shiny* objects reflect light well. Light bounces off the surface and into your eyes.

Mirror, Mirror on the wall, who's the fairest of them all?

YUK!

2) *Dull*, *dark* and *black* objects *don't* reflect light well. Light *can't* bounce off the surface.

Now do you see...

Remember, draw your light rays *straight* and make sure they start and finish *on* (not just near) the important objects. They go from the source to the eye, not the other way round. Learn your *light sources*, and remember that things like the Moon just *reflect* the Sun's light.

Making Sound

Here's all you'll need to know about sound — in just two pages. Sounds too good to be true...

1) Sound happens when Something Vibrates

1) It may be obvious what is vibrating, and making the noise.

2) Or — it may not. Here it's the air in the bottle which is vibrating to produce the noise.

2) Sounds are Transmitted through Air or Another Material

1) Vibrating objects make the air or material next to it vibrate as well. So the vibrations kind of travel *(are transmitted)* through the air.

2) Sound can travel through all kinds of materials — like stone, brick, water and glass.

3) Sound cannot travel through a vacuum — because there is nothing to transmit the vibrations.

VACUUM CHAMBER

That looks like a quiet place!!

3) We hear sounds when the Vibrating Air hits our Ear Drums

1) The *vibrating air* hits our *ear drums* and makes them vibrate.

2) This vibration is picked up by our *brains*.

OBJECT VIBRATES ⟶ AIR VIBRATES ⟶ EAR DRUM VIBRATES

Changing Sound

The More Energy in the Vibration — the LOUDER the Sound

That just means the *harder* you hit something, the *louder* the noise.
BUT — don't test this rule on your little brother — it will work, but Mum won't like it.

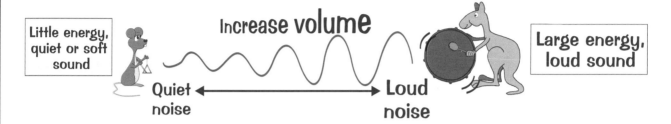

Little energy, quiet or soft sound

Increase volume

Quiet noise ⟷ Loud noise

Large energy, loud sound

The Pitch is how High or Low a Note is

1) The *shorter* the vibrating object, the *higher* the pitch of the note.

A
B

String A will give the lower note because it is longer than B

Breathe →   Breathe →

A   B

Bottle A will give a higher note because the vibrating column of air is shorter than in bottle B

2) The *larger* the vibrating object, the *lower* the pitch of the note. (*It's deeper.*)

High notes

Low notes

The Tighter the String, the Higher the Pitch of the Note

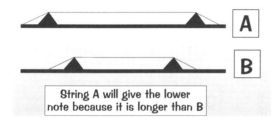 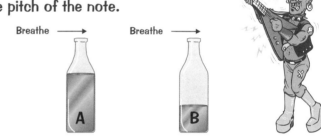

Low-pitched note   Twang   Ping   *High-pitched note*

Loose string vibrating

Tight string vibrating

This is kind of like tuning a guitar.

Now it's your turn to pitch in — and learn this lot...

As you may have noticed, *vibration* and *vibrating* are the in words on these pages, so learn them. Make sure you know *what's* vibrating to make the sound, and you need to remember that for you to hear a sound, the *air* has to vibrate and then your *ear drum* has to vibrate. Thinking about musical instruments or elastic bands will help you remember about *pitch*.

Electric Circuits

Get switched on to this — it's a powerful section.

1) We get Electricity from the Mains or from Batteries

1) Many *appliances* (*devices*) in our homes use mains electricity to work.
   Without it our lives would be *darker*, *duller* and *colder*.

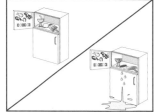

Televisions/Computers   Fridges/Freezers   Lights   Heaters

2) Smaller electrical appliances often use *batteries* which store electricity.
   These appliances can be *moved* from place to place.

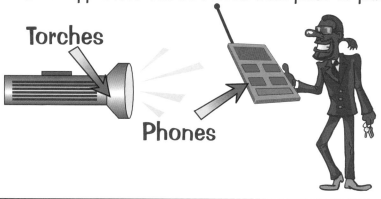

Torches

Phones

Toys

2) Electricity can be Dangerous

An electric shock from a mains socket *could kill you*. Electricity from the mains is a *lot* more powerful than electricity from a battery.

<u>*NEVER*</u>   stick scissors, pens, fingers or anything else into a mains socket.

<u>*NEVER*</u>   touch switches with wet hands.

<u>*NEVER*</u>   use electrical appliances near water.

<u>*ALWAYS*</u>   hold the plastic part of a plug when plugging in and unplugging appliances.

DANGER

HIGH VOLTAGE

3) Electricity can only Travel if there's a Complete Circuit

1) Electricity travels from the *power source*, such as a battery, around a series of *conductors* (*the circuit*) *back* to the power source.

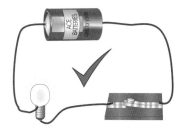

2) If there's a *gap* in the circuit *no* electricity will flow.

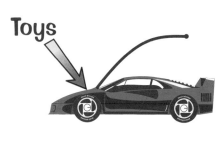

Gap

Electric Circuits

4) Circuit Diagrams use Symbols instead of Pictures

Make sure you know these symbols and components,
and use them when you're drawing circuit diagrams:

A circuit diagram showing
battery, wires, three switches,
a bulb and a buzzer.

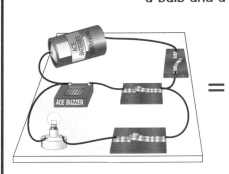 =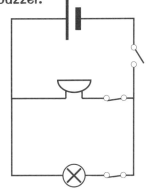

Component	Picture	Symbol
Battery(Cell)		—|⊢—
Bulb		—⊗—
Buzzer		
Motor		—Ⓜ—
Switch-off		—o⁄ o—
Switch-on		—o o—

5) The Batteries and Components must be set up Properly

Batteries and components must be put together correctly for the circuit to work.

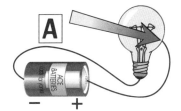

A Circuit A *won't work* because the wire
has been connected to the glass on
the bulb which is an insulator. ☹

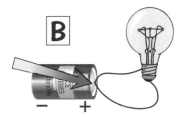

B Circuit B *won't work* because both wires are
connected to the same end of the battery. ☹

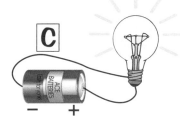

C HOORAY! Circuit C *will work*. ☺
(as long as the battery isn't flat).

Electrickery

Use symbols in circuits — but do it quietly...

This electricity stuff does look a bit complicated, eh? But it's really not that bad. Electricity
has to get from one end of the battery back to the other end of the battery for the circuit to
work. Remember, *no* electricity will flow if there's a *gap* in the circuit. Circuit diagrams use
symbols as a kind of shorthand, and yes, you *really do* need to *learn* all the symbols.

Changing Circuits

You know how to make a bulb light — well here's some more brill stuff you can do to control where the electricity goes and where it doesn't go.

1) Switches Control the Flow of Electricity in a Circuit

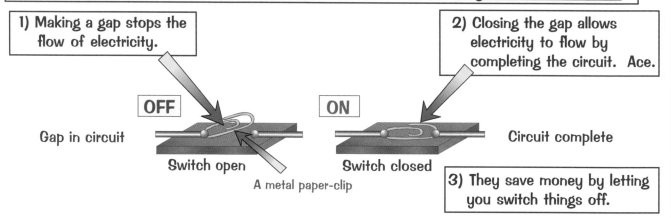

1) Making a gap stops the flow of electricity.

2) Closing the gap allows electricity to flow by completing the circuit. Ace.

OFF — Gap in circuit — Switch open — A metal paper-clip

ON — Circuit complete — Switch closed

3) They save money by letting you switch things off.

2) Switches — Control Part of a Circuit and Save Money

Take a look at the switches in these circuit diagrams — some are *open* and some are *closed*. See if you can work out which bulbs will *light*.
(Cos I'm a nice guy — I've given you the answers below.)

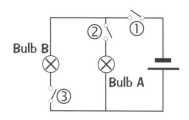

Switches ①, ② and ③ are *open*
— no current will flow.
Bulbs A and B will *NOT* light.

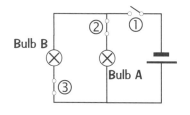

Switch ① is *open*
— so the electricity cannot flow around.
Bulbs A and B will *NOT* light.

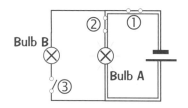

Switches ① and ② are *closed*
— so only bulb *A* lights. The red line shows where the electricity flows.

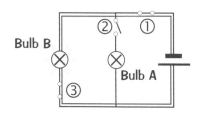

Switches ① and ③ are *closed*. This time only bulb *B* lights. The red line shows the route the electricity flows.

Remember — if the bulb is off it saves you money, and makes the bulb last longer.

Changing Circuits

Now it's time to look at some very slightly more complicated circuits *(don't panic)*.

3) Altering Simple Circuits

Starting with a simple circuit — (a battery, switch, bulb and wire), you can alter the number of batteries and the number of bulbs (but only alter one thing at a time).

Add More Batteries (in a line) — the bulb will be Brighter

"IN A LINE" is known as *"IN SERIES"*

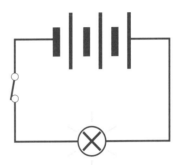

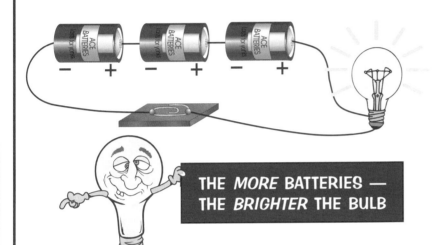

TAKE CARE THOUGH — TOO MANY BATTERIES WILL DESTROY ("BLOW") THE BULB.

THE *MORE* BATTERIES — THE *BRIGHTER* THE BULB

Add More Bulbs (in a line) — the bulbs will get Dimmer

The bulbs will be dimmer *(less bright)* than a single bulb would be in the same circuit.

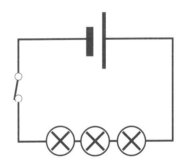

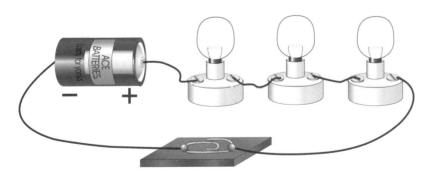

If we had three motors here instead, they'd turn slower than just one.

THE *MORE* BULBS — THE *FAINTER* THE LIGHT

Switch on your mind — but don't race around these circuits...

This stuff looks a bit more complicated, but if you think about it one step at a time then you'll get there. Remember electricity *can't flow* if there's a *gap* — that'll help you work out which bulbs will light in circuits with *switches*. The *more bulbs* you have in line in a circuit, the *dimmer* they'll all be. And don't forget, the one nearest the battery is *not* brighter — they're all the same.

Section Three — Physical Processes

Summary Questions For Section Three

Well, here it is, the page you've all been waiting for. This is where you'll find out just how well you *know* your stuff — and its all pretty important stuff too. Some of these questions may *stretch* you a bit, but you'll find all the answers somewhere in this section.

1) What is *friction?*
2) What is the *name* of the force that pulls objects *down* towards the centre of the Earth? Is there anywhere on Earth where you *don't* feel the effect of this force?
3) What *shape* are the *Sun*, *Earth* and the *Moon?*
4) What does the *Earth* orbit *around*, and how *long* does it take?
5) What does the Moon orbit *around*, and how *long* does it take?
6) Put in order of size *(biggest to smallest)* — the *Earth*, the *Moon* and the *Sun*.
7) Why does the Moon *appear* to *change shape* as it orbits the Earth?
8) *Where* is the Moon in its orbit when we cannot see it at all?
9) How long does it take for the Earth to *rotate once?*
10) What causes *day* and *night?*
11) Is it night-time for *all parts* of the world at the *same time?*
12) Does the *Sun* move around the Earth?
13) Which of the following statements is true, a) or b)?

     a) We see an object when light from our eyes hits that object.

     b) We see an object when light from that object hits our eyes.

14) *Where* does the Sun appear to *rise* and *set?*
15) How are *sounds* produced?
16) Name *one* thing that sound can't travel through and explain why not.
17) *How* could you make the stretched skin on a drum give out a *higher* note?
18) Why do *bathroom* light switches often have a cord hanging from them?

19) Name three electrical components used in simple circuits.
20) Draw a *circuit diagram* showing a circuit with:

       two batteries, wires, an open switch and a buzzer.

21) Draw a circuit diagram to show how *switches* can be used to control two different parts of a circuit.
22) How would you make a bulb in a circuit shine with a *fainter* light? Suggest *two* ways to do this.

Index

Index

Answers to Summary Questions

Section One

1) Movement, reproduction, nutrition, and growth.
2) a) incisors b) molars c) canines.
3) Four from: Brushing teeth twice a day, flossing teeth, drinking water with fluoride, visiting the dentist regularly, eating the right foods.
4) Starches, sugars, proteins, fats, vitamins, fibre and water.
5) Exercise strengthens the muscles, develops the lungs, helps body co-ordination, uses up food and can help you sleep.
6) Smoking causes lung cancer, alcohol damages the liver.
7) The heart.
8) The blood takes oxygen away and gives carbon dioxide back.
9) The windpipe.
10) For support, to protect delicate organs, to allow movement.
11) It relaxes.
12) Birth, childhood, adolescence, adulthood, old age and death.
13) Leaves, roots, stem, flower.
14) In the flower.
15) A pollen grain.
16) A seed starting to grow.
17) Habitat.
18) Long roots, fleshy stems and thin leaves (needles).
19) One from: Long tail and large toes, large ears, thin fur, active at night.
20) One from: Streamlined body, small ears, layers of fat, oily fur or webbed feet.
21) "Is food for."
22) Plants.
23) Producers, other consumers.
24) a = Glenn, b = Kate, c = Edward, d = Chris, e = Paul, f = Lucy, g = Pam, h = Nick
25) Germs.
26) Yeast is used to make bread and beer; some bacteria are used to make vinegar, cheese and yoghurt; bacteria rot dead organisms and put nutrients into the soil.
27) Vaccinations and antibiotics
28) Without protection lots of living organisms would die out.

Section Two

1) It is strong.
2) Metals.
3) Something that won't let heat pass through it easily.
4) a) no b) yes c) no.
5) No - some are harder, some are permeable.
6) Lets water pass through.
7) Solids, liquids, gases.
8) a) reversible, b) irreversible, c) reversible, d) irreversible
9) They evaporate as it gets warmer.
10) Leave the solution in a wide dish in a warm place.
11) Water evaporates from the sea, condenses and falls as rain over the land and runs back down to the sea.
12) a) filter paper b) magnet c) sieve d) spoon (with heat).
13) Any 3 of: wood, coal, oil, gas, charcoal, etc...
14) They must burn.
15) Food.

Section Three

1) Force between things that are touching.
2) Gravity. No, it's felt everywhere.
3) Spherical/ballshaped
4) The Sun, 1 year/365¼ days
5) The Earth, 28 days.
6) Sun, Earth, Moon.
7) We see different amounts of the Moon's sunny side as it orbits the Earth.
8) Between Sun and Earth (an eclipse); or new Moon; or on the other side of the Earth.
9) 1 day.
10) The Sun shines on one part of the Earth.
11) No.
12) No, it stays at the centre of the solar system.
13) b
14) It appears to rise in the east, and to set in the west.
15) Something vibrates.
16) Vacuum – nothing to vibrate.
17) Make it tighter.
18) So you can't touch the switch with wet hands.
19) Bulb, buzzer, motor.
20) Fewer batteries, more bulbs, longer wire.
21) Any correct answer is OK, here's one example:

22) Add more bulbs; if there's more than one battery in the circuit, you could remove one or more batteries.